The Hill

The Hill

Angela France

Nine
Arches
Press

The Hill
Angela France

ISBN: 9781911027218

Cover and jacket illustrations: 'The King's Touch' © Fumio Obata
www.fumioobata.co.uk

Map on page 6 by Caro McIntosh, University of Gloucestershire
cartographer.

First published July 2017 by:

Nine Arches Press
PO Box 6269
Rugby
CV21 9NL
United Kingdom

www.ninearchespress.com

Printed in the United Kingdom by Imprint Digital

Nine Arches Press is supported using public funding by the
National Lottery through Arts Council England.

Supported using public funding by
**ARTS COUNCIL
ENGLAND**

For 'The Leckhampton Stalwarts'
and all those who fight for the land

Leckhampton Hill, 1902

Contents

"Don't steal the goose from the common, or you will get jail, but steal the common from the goose, and you will be let off without a stain on your character"
– William Sparrow, 1902

Voices found on the hill

loads of mad quarry bits   up by Devil's Chimney

    a fabulous limestone outcrop   overlooking Cheltenham

easy dirt tracks   technical climbs   swooping singletrack

    Yellowhammers Bullfinches Linnets Goldcrests

charged on remand   with breaking   destroying a fence

to the amount   of 10/-   property of the Quarries Company

    purchased by Mr H.J. Dale

    Common Rock Rose Wild Thyme Autumn Gentian Orchid

limestone clay spackled face paint   the whoops coming back down

    Foxes Shrews Hedgehogs Moles Bats and Badgers.

the cliffs in the quarry are choss   top outs are bad

    it was determined   by a large body of men

that Cratchley's   cottage must be removed

exposure of the whole   Lower Inferior Oolite formation

    one outcrop area   we further give you notice

    warn you and your servants

Chiffchaffs Willow Warblers Grasshopper Warblers and Tree Pipits

a boxing competition   between Charlton and Leckhampton men

head over to Seven Springs   down that spooky valley

range through oncolites sandy limestones and oolites

Wood Mice Field Voles Grey Squirrels Rabbits and Roe and Muntjac

good paths to this promontory Iron Age hill fort

a Trig Surface Block   music and dancing   play my harp

on the hill on Good Friday

Slow Worms Common Lizards Adders Buzzard Sparrowhawk Kestrel

Landslip

I wake in fog, my long bones feeling stone
in their marrow   water-laden air collects
on rock and leaf, shines lichen to glow
and glisten   an unseen moon reflects
from droplets   slides down the slopes
a light that hides   trees after years of
growing erect   bend and melt invisible
this bowl in the wood has been my place
for so long   now strange to me   I stand
in an opaque globe   snatches of sound
pierce the veil   near then far   clear then
muffled   a child laughs   a wooden ball
thuds   fierce men shout   a fiddle plays
my torch is baffled by reflection   only
shivers of movement disturb the mist   a
half-seen shadow might be a huddle of
women or a bramble   time and fog
merge into blindness   I turn around
brittle leaves crumbling   under my feet
I can smell herbs lemons   farther up the
hill harp notes weave and drop like first
hints of rain   a dog barks   runs by me
disappears   a chain released

Nadder speaks

         stonestuff listens
on woodside and hillside
in the delverns and pits
yellow-stone sunders
and splits   falls to bend
man-shaped iron.
Nadder speaks
      to wort-cropper
and wold-mouse   hareling
and leafworm   says
hide yourself at sun-time
yeartide   when man sets
forehold on paths in woods
and grasses   takes tithing
through world-all
               show yourself
to the unkithed child
who sits wisefast and seaving
under trees

Trails and Ways I

I used to think the cottage should be mine
when I scrambled up the steep track
which climbed from the pit behind

through beeches whose roots widen cracks
in the stone beneath the hill's gaunt skin
where clumps of hart's tongue lie like green rags.

I would have lived there, content within
its squat walls with a dog at my heel
and no sense then of how adults must live

between wage and want, and want and need.
I stand at the fence to see the cottage again;
my feet in the metalled litter of beech leaves

and my back to the hollow where trees and dense
scrub hide the remains of iron plates
that guided rumbling drams on a cabled ascent.

The King's Touch

The King of the Common has quartz in his eyes,
etched into lines on his face. He crouches
in limestone fissures to watch the rain shine

stone to gold, toes gravel into rivulets as gullies
deepen. He feels the stone's thirst under his feet,
hears water trickling down through caves and layers

of time, dripping from fossils and faults, soaking
down to the bedrock which once heaved
and bucked to push these gaunt cliffs high

above the valley. He sits on top when rain stops,
tracks the old paths by sight. He can forgive
the short-lived tramlines that cut sharp lines

down the hill, the ragged outcrops they left
standing, the faded echoes of the drum's
rattle and clang as the trams scaled the scarp.

He grants a king's pardon to scrub and gorse
for narrowing paths, smiles on the beeches
that stretch up from gravel-pits for the sun.

The cliffs crack and crumble at his will, he heel-jabs
the edge to send stones down to rattle and bounce
in bicycle wheels when boys build ramps on old ways.

He can't forgive tarmac and brick, the houses
encrusting the low slopes; broods on the weight
held in the cliff, on what a rolling boulder could do.

Dale bought the quarries then
claimed to own the soil of the
hill   the paths where working
people walked   the pits where
children played   Sparrow says
don't steal a goose from the
common or you will get jail
but steal the common from the
goose and be let off   without a
stain on your character

Map Reading

I hold the old map in mind as I walk, speak
the path-names aloud to myself, try
to visualise the angles where they meet.

In the woods I am unsure; trees and scrub deny
the map. I don't know whether I tread skew path
or bottom jenny, can't see where the path-edge lies

under hart's tongue and tree-roots that clasp
onto crumbling stone. A hundred years of growth
has greened the hill and healed the marks

of quarries and the trams which rose
up the scarp. Back then, those who walked
here needed no map. A rich man's boast

that he'd close the hill because he'd bought
the stone led to maps drawn and re-drawn,
hard-working men in jail and taken to court

for going where they'd always gone.
They'd hobnailed the way to villages over the top,
and knew which path late-to-school children would run;

they named the paths but saw no need to plot
on paper. They went where generations did, obeyed
the curves and lines of the hill. I should drop

the need to get it right, call where I tread the way.

Hauke sees

allworld from the wind-eye
  has no ruth
      for hareling nor wold-mouse
         coney nor dove
sees them bespeak out of shelterness
  shrithing through long-leaf
falls eyeblink-swift to hend
  and sunder   to take his tithe

Hauke has no meanlust
        no nithecraft
needful only to ride the sky
    Hauke is hauke-worth
        Hauke is

Calling the Witnesses

The aged witnesses grumble over the hill,
stop to point at narrowed paths and fallen trees.
Hawker kicks at encroaching roots while Bill Tilling

beats down an earth-packed ramp, prods the debris
and asks how a man can carry bread on the stoneway
to Cubberly and Cowley when young men speed

down the trails on bikes, making fresh ruts every day
to catch a foot or twist a knee. Sparrow Hiscock
climbs past the quarry to Devil's Chimney, waylays

walkers who follow the signposted way along the top,
demands to know where his garden went. His staff
points at the rocky slope below, the treacherous drop

where he says he grew cabbage and spuds, the path
to his cottage gone under fallen boulders and moss.
Dorothy Trye's skirts wick damp from the long grass

as she leaves the skew path to find the way across
to Seven Springs. She can't find the Ladies' College girls
and misses the company, the giggle and scoff

of bright voices, the ground-covering chatter and twirl
of their youth. She's fading now, blending into the cliffs
behind her; Trye, Tilling, Hiscock, no more than blurred

statements, archived names on a list.

Remembrance

The seat at the edge of the beech wood is a rough-hewn slab
on two blocks, overlooking a steep slope where volunteers

have been burning scrub to preserve rare grasses.
A plaque suggests Rest and Be Thankful; the name below

is nothing to me but I'll sit and borrow someone else's dead
while I look over treetops to the town winking in sunlight

and consider my own. Ashes have been left in a garden
of remembrance or taken for scattering in favourite places.

I have dead across miles and across oceans, dear to me,
but feel no need to carve a name or kneel by a grave.

This is perhaps a lacking in me, a failure to honour
those who have gone. Or it is a remembering

of the first time I saw someone dead; a familiar face
still warm, a lamp's reflection in not-fully-closed eyes,

but an undeniable absence of person, an emptiness,
nothing attached to the name, no-one there.

Sparrow says men from Bath Road
hide in the garden   crouch behind
brassicas skulk in rhubarb crowns
Dale's men waiting for king's men
cudgels and sticks   fists and boots
armed to belabour us when we set
foot on the path   Sparrow writes
the letters tells the world   Sparrow
says the world don't listen   says the
press are *fustian and flapdoodle*   no
friends of the hill

Trails and Ways II

An old woman leans on the car-park gate,
wiry hair springing from under her waxed hat,
a grey-muzzled collie stands at her knee, another's laid

at her feet. She sees me looking and snaps
a wink at me; *they tore the cottage down once,*
for being in the way, every stone and scrap.

She tells me her grandpa was amongst
the men who marched from town
Up hill to down Dale, whose response

to fences and blocked paths was to pound
on walls, to harden hands and voices,
to lead hundreds of feet over disputed ground.

Aged Witness #3: Sparrow Hiscock

I have walked on the hill as long as I've been alive. I was sent to learn the baker-trade from Isaac Crump. I was young and strong, carrying bread to customers over the hill and no wagoner nor squire stopped me on tramway path or stoneway. I followed the common wall track to Cubberley then to Cowley over the hill top by Hartley Bottom. Dale's no right. He's wrong to think he'll ban us from our hill. We've always walked here and we'll be there Easter; with our donkey rides and music, celebrating the people's will.

Brock says

delve deep
      under stone
claw sharpstrike into roots
           and earth
find allworld below
      for shelterness

my jaws make a hallowing
of sinless worm and slug

I am needful of night-swart
uncleft in my woodside ledemark

leave sun-tide
      to aquern and wort-cropper
           beingless to me

Footfall

There is no grass here, no ground elder
or violet. Trees cling to rock-studded soil,
shaded by the pitch of the scarp, roots knotted
on the surface. Only the moss is green, softening
broken branches, making alien of old stumps.

The ground demands attention. This is no place
for wandering or wool-gathering, no distracted
tramping while you filter memories through a sieve
of words. Each footfall must be felt, judged safe,
as beech masts, jagged stones, and a litter
of last year's leaves shift and slip on the steep sides
of the pit. Saplings offer hand-sized support for you
to hold in place, not ready to head all the way down.

they called him king   when he put
fire in their heads and tired bones
let it blaze in their voices   spill from
fingertips   boots scorch green to
black   as fences trample down to
matchwood wire hauls away from
hasty posts the burn in men's arms
drives pickaxes against stone   turns
weariness to ember   a woman's
skirt brushes against piled furniture
sets it aflame   the king stands
it's right   it's right   it's our right

Fences

stepping out from woods   into the clearing
footstep shocked short   a new fence
heart high   dulled silver sculpted points
curved inwards   alien against stone   a
gate   double-chained weighted a padlock
for safety for erosion   no more clambering
crumbling walls slipping down   a ramp
once was steps   I am divided by brushed
steel points   wanting it preserved as my
memory   wanting it free   other fences
once   pulled up broken down   raged into
matchwood   the man they called king said
I'm off to fight for what I'm not allowed to walk
over   wrote from the trenches barbed-
wire its likeness to fenced hill-paths the
new fence is rigid   locked   into the ground
trees grow   fissures in a quarry-face shift
and spread   rocks fall and roll   fences fail

Aged Witness #5: Dorothea Trye

My family owned the hill before Dale. He knew people would walk up on Sundays. Good Friday they'd head off the trails to the pits, set up stalls and games, music, boxing, lemonade. Sometimes people would ride empty drams up to the cable entry for larks. I recall one girl claimed it Grandfather's fault she fell out and almost got her nose cut off. She ran to him, but he sewed it straight back on, quite nicely. I've seen her out, about the town, and think her mended nose looks fine, the stitching hardly shows. She's no reason for complaining; he helped her without blame and drams weren't there to be misused.

Trails and Ways III

Helix Pomatia

Hail, Creamy-shelled long-foot,
antennae-questing rain-lover. You step lightly
on this place; settled on the limestone slopes,
sleeping deep in the tussocks through the day,
showing yourself slowly, shyly, on dew-laden mornings.
How carefully, carefully, you dug with your soft head
to winter in the earth below frost-scarred grasses.
Your shell lightens each year; it's spring
and here you are, slowing my feet on the path
across the grasslands, reminding
me to watch where I tread.

Miss Beale sent a hundred girls from
school to the hill   to tramp the
old paths in twos and threes   to
behave as ladies   to trespass where
Dale would deny them   to take
their air and exercise   Miss Beale
wrote letters   sent Dale's pianos out
of her school,   displeased.

Tuneless

When the pianos went from the school
dust fell silently on the spaces they left.
The music teacher sat facing the wall,
clasped her hands to stop her fingers
                    spreading an octave.

Hymns at morning assemblies stuttered
and staggered through the melody, slipped
sharp, then as flat as the baby-grand-shaped
space on the stage. The principal tried
to lead, faltered as the girls dawdled.

Unfaded rectangles of carpet marked
the boarding houses; girls stepped round them,
whispered over bedtime hot chocolate, hushed
every chink or rattle of spoon on cup.

In the old quarry, a man turns a small block
 in his hands, smoothes dust from ivory
with his thumb, tosses it back into rubble,
bends back to work, whistling.

Trails and Ways IV

Don't climb the rock face in Wagon Quarry,
where deep fissures divide limestone into boulders
which could fall under a sparrow's foot or wing's flurry.

Take the scrubby side where a path twists round alder,
hawthorn, seems to vanish under brambles,
slips under scree but will take you over the shoulder

to the plain on the hilltop where the wind dandles
grass from green to silver and fox-trails
criss-cross under a wide sky while a kestrel untangles

air currents and waits for movement, a chance of prey.
Bypass the Iron-Age mounds and take a left
past Devil's Chimney on an incline built for rails,

steep and smooth for feet; dig heels into every dint and cleft
to stay upright, down to Deadman's Quarry where stone slabs
lay where they fell, and rolled, and came to rest.

Great cracks in the cliff-face suggest caves and trapped
secrets to a child seeking fossils or beetles,
asks how deep into the golden stone a crabwise

step might reach. Shadows of dusty people
drift around rusty iron bent in mysterious shapes
and scars on the stone from drum-drawn cable.

Aged Witness #8: William Tilling

I looked after my father's sheep when he rented land on the top. People used the paths daily, and were never stopped. Weekly marketing, men to work, schoolboys scuffing feet. William Hawkes supplied donkeys for those who wished to ride up the steep paths. Some young women thought it fun to ride up sitting in the panniers, till the beast shied and they took a spill. Good Fridays, travelling men came with games and stalls; there was music and contests, a break from workaday lives. We bought our wives catchpenny trinkets and police watched nearby to see no damage was done. I'd climb up the skew path and play my harp by middle jenny.

The Harp

The shepherd's harp is cradled in oilcloth,
stands in the corner away from the fire.
Its paint is cracked, scuffed on the corners
of the sound box where once-gilt scrolls
fade into shadows. He's told it is a lap harp,
not a Welsh harp as it has no high head
and the wrong shape for a lute harp.
He only knows it fits on to his back
when he walks over the hills and sings
to his fingers when he strokes the strings.

it was submitted that to be a riot
someone must be terrified the
Cratchleys ran   the cottage
walls lay in heaps of stone   and
the Cratchleys ran   outbuildings
burned to ash   clothes smouldered
in the trampled garden   the
Cratchleys ran but   *there were no
unnecessary circumstances of disorder*

Echoes

on the hillside   my hand turns copper leaves on
the ground   measuring their seasons through
the trees   the car park   bright colours wink
catch the light   the stone cottage below me
stands foursquare   its garden creeping up the
slope   defended behind fences   from trees
leaning in   the walls seem to have grown
in place   little changed from old pictures
only a car pulled onto the tramway   a new
greenhouse brings it to now   hard to imagine
it as rubble   smashed down by anger and right
a woman told me of a night   she was woken
by rumbling   screeching   shouts and crashes
she said it was a certain time of year   an echo
perhaps   of a cable breaking   a quarry truck
racketing down the hill   upturning in fields
below   young lives lost   if I sit long enough
wait for the uncertainties of dusk to fall
when edges and outlines   fade and sounds
shiver   bounce off the trees   echoes may
falter up the slope   shouts   jeers a shudder
of axe on stone   crackle and spit of flame
splintering wood   a wave of fury crashing
against cottage walls   a roar as they fall

Trails and Ways V

Lepus europaeus

Dew-dabbler, dancer,
trickster in flight,
your inky-tipped ears
point a glamour on morning.
Moon-jumper, mist-still,
crafty deceiver,
your bright wary eye winks
a veil past the way.
Heart-stopper, flash-tail,
master of spells,
your long feet left prints
in the centre of my chest.

Shroud

On this greened hill   where nails
   fixed iron plates to stone   where oil

   and fire scoured vetch and violet
from earth   where clang and rattle

drove small creatures to ground
                moss forgives

moss blurs snow-like   blends
        angles into curves   cloaks straight lines

soothes   the scar in the stone   the split rock
   the broken branch   the felled tree

moss covers the rail   cushions the footprint
                        forgives

Aged Witness #11: William Ballinger

My father was a Cleeve tenant, Leckhampton was owned by the Squire. My father was driver on a load of stone, an errand he'd to do most days. His horses went on Lower Stoneway without bidding, so used were they to the routes they took. Squire Trye came by, astride his big hunter and straight away began to whip the foremost horse on father's wagon to turn it, saying the Stoneway was private. Father jumped down and laid his whip on Trye at which the Squire galloped off. Father thought he'd be in trouble with the law but nothing happened; it made him sure that old rights could not be lost.

Balancing Point

The path on the crest holds a balance
between scarp and slope, runs a line
from hardly-there mounds where a people
lived in skins and circles to the crumble
of long quiet quarry-edge. Scrubby trees
cling to the brink, roots reaching in air,
netting stones, clumps of moss, dry earth.

Your feet on the path are unsteady, sensing
the fulcrum's fine point. You can only stand,
bracing against history's breath as it bends
grass and whips trees. Figures pass,
unfocussed, they could be wearing skins
or waterproofs, tweed or polar fleece.
From the edge, sight stretches across the valley,
you watch your own past swirl as mist.
Step back, step back. Walk on.

Fox

is my namen
    man slurs me elles
  clithe not to my ruddy hide
my ledemark tithing is all
  the dun I tread
     coneys and wort-croppers
are underyoke to me
  bow to my holyroom
    under delvern and root

niht-time is mine   evenleether
with brock and nadder
   leafworm and wanderlight
my wif is a bale-fire at swart-time
  calling wellstemned

I wend where I will
   seave and rede
     fox is my namen

Trails and Ways VI

Someone has capped the engine-house walls
with concrete to slow their determined falling down;
it sits on the yellow stone like a smooth grey shawl

but fails to stop the crumbling to ground.
Across the clearing the lime-kiln platform still stands,
steps worn to treachery, pillars like sarsens bound

in ivy and lichen, crumbling under buddleia plants
through time, and falling cliff, and climbing feet.
Campfire circles mark the ground, leave brands

of smoke trails and rusty scars on the stone; some neatly
cleared, others a jumble of bent cutlery and scorched cans.
I see them on summer mornings, sleepy teens

up here to spend a night away from the adult glance,
to swear and smoke, to posture and flirt and try
for more, to drink all they can carry and try to expand

their taste for anything they think they can later deny.
The girls, who last night were giggles and make-up and hope,
are pale and bad-tempered walking down under the morning sky,

not expecting the steepness of the downward slope.

the king's away   gone to
London in a Black Maria
for making a stand   the
stalwarts swear to keep his
place   he's a working man
a poor man   a brickworks
clay-digger   a strong man
a fierce man   no money for
law   or lawyer   public
appeals   lists of donations
he stood for your rights   for
the paths   for the hill

Timeless

From the hilltop, the town glitters a little in late sun,
encrusted on the valley floor like quartz in a rock pool.
This is my town. I know its streets, all its many changes,
though from here the wink and glint of streetlights
suggests the permanence of gemstone. Buildings crumble
or grow, roads roll back on themselves to widen or fall
away; regret has no currency and time lets nothing be.

Up here on the edge, with traces of Iron-Age works
behind me and the wind bending yellowing grass
round my ankles and a buzzard wheeling overhead,
I could call this place timeless but I'd be lying.
The land wears time as a mantle, bending briars
over paths, growing trees to fill a slope, change
encoded in every seed and speck of earth.

Aged Witness #7 Thomas Hawkes

Off the skew-path there were garden patches, they grew turnips and oats where there's soil, not the rocky slope. The Quarrymen let them; Harding had one, Sparrow Hiscock, Morden. People would ramble all over but it was dangerous closer by the quarries. One lady's dog was lost by falling from the rocks. She said she'd sue but Squire told her he'd notices along the way, warning of the hazardous cliffs but she left the trail and he'd not accept any blame. He said any fault of his was outweighed by her not having taught the mutt to read. She was upset but she'd chosen to leave the path. His daft reasons stung, but he made her retract.

Trails and Ways VII

Vipera berus

Beware their secret ways,
           their shy hiding
     in the tangle of hawthorn
           where you look
               for a dog's lost ball
    or under the rock
        you lift in search of ammonites.
Watch for muscled coils,
      zig-zag back,
          tongue flicker
               to taste
                  your approach.
     There's no malice,
           no intent.
The strike and sting of their fangs
      only means
          you're in their way.

The Wall

On the hilltop, where scarp gentles
into farmland, a banner hangs
along a crumbling wall.
Traditional Country Crafts
  Learn Dry Stone Walling
A group stands, learning, earnest
in bright-coloured jackets, work gloves
clenched in white hands.

The instructor is talking,
turning a large stone in his hands,
showing the shape, the edge,
how it snicks into the space
it was meant to fit. He beckons
a man forward, asks him to feel
the stone's fit, how it won't rock
or shift, how it is become wall.

I think of a man I knew once.
A waller by trade until disease
took his sight. He knew how
to set a cheek-end four square,
how the tie-stones know
their right place. He told me
how social workers spoke
of long canes and dogs,
of re-training and computers.

He spread out his big hands,
calloused and strong.
What can I do, he said
What can I do?

the king returned from jail
king no more   the town
turned its back   on his
rage the stalwarts   stood
on the cart   photographed
grim   Ma Ballinger   in
front   white   apron
starched   solid by her son
holding his pipe   hatless
a small dog looks on

Wort-cropper

twitches swart-tips
    unbeheld   hallows world-all
seaves shelterness in the wold
by woodside
    is lovesome to leafworm
hickle and wold-mouse

but afraid of hunger-bitten fox
    and loathes foesome man
who tears world-all to wanhope

Naming

Some time in my middle years
I needed to know the names of things.
For so many years I walked this path
in the woods before I knew these leaves
as dog's mercury or that white star
as wood anemone.
                    It is as if the naming
of things will slow the earth's spin,
fix my feet to the ground.
I tell myself as I walk,
that is mallow, vetch, viper's bugloss;
a smoky bracket fungus on the fallen
paper birch. This delicate shell
a heath snail, that high keening
a sparrow hawk.
                    The seasons are harder
to name; is this spring, or the beginning
of summer? I will know
                    when winter comes.

Trails and Ways VIII

The boy looks familiar, one of the Dales,
I think. He stands on his pedals as he blasts
down the ramp, skids his wheels on shale

to stop before me. He's armoured in plastic,
face raw-boned under lime-dust and mud spatter,
shins black-greaved like wing cases.

You can't walk there, it's not a footpath,
just a crossing point between trails.
He says I might be knocked down if I go on past.

Under my feet are fox-prints, roots, iron nails,
thin soil studded with foreign stone,
rocks scored in lines from long-gone rails.

Behind me a platform, mossy and overgrown
where lime kilns rose; where a child
could see crumbling pillars as a temple of gold.

Sparrows in the whitethorn present their wild
experiments in verse and line, work-a-day brown
feathers flit in the green, a flashed wing, a tipped tail.

The boy rides on down, heels digging in as he rounds
the curves of the trail, speed building on the incline.
I go on up, my feet on the path claiming the ground.

Wilding

Everything under my feet has been named
at some time. Bryophytes and lichens,
liverworts and vetch. The narrow paths carry
their own names, know when they were routes
to work or school. At the crest, a faded board
labels the view, names directions, hills, rivers.

A broken tree leans on its neighbour, branches
rotting on the ground, given up to beetles, fungi,
mould. Moss creeps to cover the break,
cushions jagged edges, lays claim over bark.
Ash, Fraxinus excelsior, its name
folded into every ring of the grain.
A trail is narrowed by whitethorn scrub,
blocked with fallen rocks, Inferior Oolite,
fractured from the cliff-face.

If we could learn a radical forgetting,
forget taxonomy, genus and species, forget
common and regional names, let trees
scribe their own language into the grain, let fungi
bloom unlabelled, let beetles burrow into soft wood
unburdened, we could let wilding be.

Greed

Fine days bring families out to chatter
up the main paths, children hopping
over gullies carved in rain. Couples saunter
with smiles and matching boots, fingers
entwined and shoulders bumping.
All the battles for rights here, the risking
of lives and liberty, and I am greedy for cloud.
I want a buffeting wind or bitter drizzle,
squelching mud or slick ice on the paths.
I want to walk away from the main track
and hear no voices. I want a lonely dawn
or to sit at the top and watch the creeping dusk.
I want to be selfish, greedy, alone.

Cold Comfort

There is a comfort in shortening days,
in dark-at-five and damp roads shining.
Rain on the window whispers permission
to bolt the door and let the curtains sigh
along the rail. Outside, the pressure's low
and the moon's demands are muffled
in cloud. A rose bush, straggled with age,
taps at the glass and an ill-fitted door
knocks a little, now and again.
It's not quite cold enough to light the fire
but I'll do it anyway, lay the kindling
across paper, rattle coal from the scuttle,
wait for the crackle and draw. Nothing
is happening, no-one is calling
and I'm glad of the night, the rain.

First Footing

When I first climbed here alone
in my tenth summer, I took pleasure
in geography-class knowledge that it's Jurassic
limestone and not a hill but an escarpment.
I turned rocks in the quarry to look for ammonites,
dreamed of dinosaur bones, lay under trees
to see saddles on stag beetles jousting with twigs.
The stone engine-house and workings were ruined
castles where I peopled kingdoms and hoped
to see the adders from the painted *Beware* signs.

So many days I trekked up the old tramway
which bent away from the road and climbed
behind the houses to emerge where I had to stand
and daydream, a little, at the cottage nestled
under the beech wood. I trailed narrow paths,
made a crypt under great roots where a pit-edge
crumbled away, and studied lichen for secret runes.
The dog at my side as I wandered the scarp
was intended to protect a child alone
but I'd already met the dangers there.
I didn't know then that like the adder,
the habit of solitude hides risk under attraction.

and Nadder says

stonestuff still listens
  when man sets forehold
on delverns and paths
   but hold sparefulness
       ware seethcraft
under ways and trails
  older wit than yours
      is undergrown

Nadder sees your meanlust
     your scrape and welt
and waits
    all things will uncleft
       in time

Litany for a Hillside

What made this path?
    Black-shelled boys on bikes, skidding
        downhill, heels gouging the bends
What made this path?
    Children dragging cardboard up the slope,
        squealing and tumbling the slide down
What made this path?
    Walking boots, dogs' paws
        criss-crossing from rabbit hole to tree
What made this path?
    Men in workboots at 6am,
        the morning-slog up to the quarry
What made this path?
    Iron rails, heavy horses,
        rickety drams bowing under stone
What made this path?
    Hundreds of feet, tearing
        down fences and clearing old rights
What made this path?
    Foxes trotting home at dawn,
        black-stockinged feet damp with dew